EXPLORING OUR SOLAR SYSTEM

THE STARS

GLOWING SPHERES IN THE SKY

DAVID JEFFERIS

Crabtree Publishing Company

www.crabtreebooks.com

▪ THE STARS

Look up at the sky on a clear night and you can see the stars. They seem to be countless, but even the sharpest human eyes cannot make out more than 3,000 or so.

Each and every one of those pinpoints glows with amazing heat. Our own Sun is a star too, and is about average for size, age, and the amount of heat it gives out. Far out in space, there are other kinds of stars including tiny stars, giant stars, stars grouped in twos and threes, and exploding stars.

In this book you can discover all about them!

Crabtree Publishing Company

PMB 16A,
350 Fifth Avenue, Suite 3308
New York, NY 10118

616 Welland Avenue,
St. Catharines, Ontario
L2M 5V6

Published by Crabtree
Publishing Company
© 2009

Written and produced by:
    David Jefferis/Buzz Books

Educational advisor: Julie Stapleton

Science advisor: Mat Irvine FBIS

Editor: Ellen Rodger

Copy editor: Adrianna Morganelli,
    Katherine Berti

Proofreader: Crystal Sikkens

Project editor: Robert Walker

Prepress technician: Margaret Amy Salter

Production coordinator: Margaret Amy Salter

▪ ACKNOWLEDGEMENTS

We wish to thank all those people who have helped to create this publication. Information and images were supplied by:

Agencies and organizations:
    ESA European Space Agency
    HST Hubble Space Telescope
    JPL Jet Propulsion Laboratory
    NASA National Aeronautics and
        Space Administration
    Spitzer images Courtesy NASA/JPL-Caltech
    Stellarium open source software

Collections and individuals:
    Alpha Archive
    Greg Dinderman/Sky & Telescope magazine
    iStockPhoto/Spectral Design
    David Jefferis
    NASA/David Hardy, Adolf Schaller

© 2009 David Jefferis/Buzz Books

Library and Archives Canada Cataloguing in Publication
Jefferis, David
    The stars : glowing spheres in the sky / David Jefferis.

(Exploring our solar system)
Includes index.
ISBN 978-0-7787-3726-1 (bound).–ISBN 978-0-7787-3743-8 (pbk.)

    1. Stars–Juvenile literature. I. Title. II. Series: Exploring our solar system (St. Catharines, Ont.)

QB801.7.J43 2008   j523.8   C2008-907015-1

Library of Congress Cataloging-in-Publication Data
Jefferis, David.
    The stars : glowing spheres in the sky / David Jefferis.
        p. cm. – (Exploring our solar system)

Includes index.
    ISBN 978-0-7787-3743-8 (pbk. : alk. paper) – ISBN 978-0-7787-3726-1 (reinforced lib. bdg. : alk. paper)
    1. Stars–Juvenile literature. I. Title. II. Series.

QB801.7.J44 2009
523.8–dc22
                                        2008046250

CONTENTS

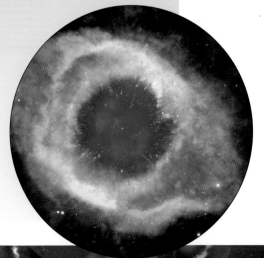

■ WHAT IS A STAR?

A star is a huge ball of hot, glowing gases such as hydrogen **and** helium.
The nearest star—the Sun—gives heat and light to our planet.

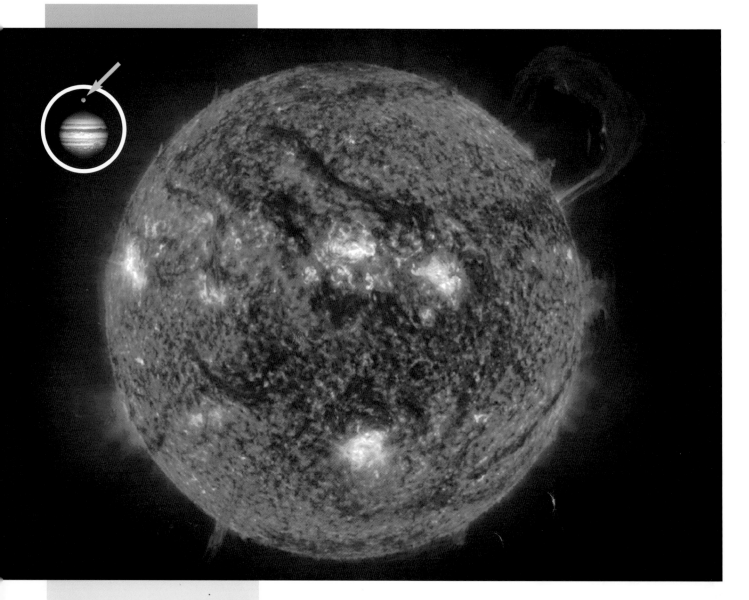

■ **Compared with the planets in our** solar system, **the Sun is huge! Shown in the circle to scale are Jupiter, the biggest planet, and the much smaller Earth (arrowed).**

■ IS THE SUN DIFFERENT FROM OTHER STARS?

All stars are different, just as no two planets are exactly the same. The Sun is good to study because it is close to us and is not too large or old. By looking at the Sun we can learn about other stars and how they work.

■ HOW DOES THE SUN SHINE SO BRIGHTLY?

The hidden secret to the power of the Sun—or any star—lies deep in the **core**, or center, where temperatures reach more than 27 million °F (15 million °C). Under this enormous heat and pressure, a process called **nuclear fusion** happens. **Atoms** of hydrogen fuse, or join together, to make helium. As they do so, huge amounts of energy are given off.

■ The Sun is a hot furnace of energy. Powerful magnetic fields, caused by fusion, swirl in and around it.

Like all stars, the Sun's energy is given off as radiation. Some radiation we feel as heat, some we see as light. Other radiation, such as X-rays, are invisible to us.

■ HOW DOES THE ENERGY REACH THE SURFACE?

Heat from a star's core moves outward quite slowly. Energy being made inside the Sun at this moment will not appear as heat and light at the surface for thousands of years. However, it is a steady process, as the Sun has been burning for about 4.6 billion years. It should burn for another 5 billion years.

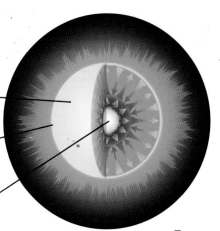

Photosphere, or surface

The Sun is 870,000 miles (1.4 million km) wide

Core, where fusion happens

■ HOW DO STARS FORM?

Stars are born in deep space, inside huge clouds of gas and dust. Star-making is a continuous process. We can see stars being formed today in gas clouds called nebulas.

WOW!
Space distances are measured in **light years**. This is the distance that light travels in a year. A light year is nearly six trillion miles (ten trillion km).

■ WHAT DOES A NEBULA LOOK LIKE?

Nebulas are among the most beautiful sights in the night sky. Through a powerful telescope, they appear as distant clouds of dusty gases that swirl in strange, twisting shapes.

Deep within the clouds, material comes together to form hot, dense blobs of matter. These blobs eventually form stars that "switch on" to start glowing with their own heat and light.

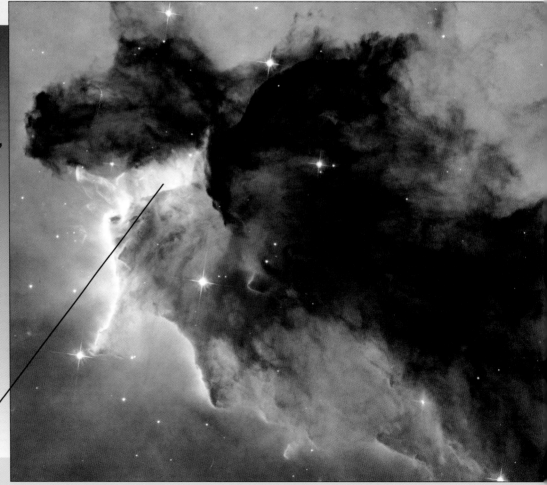

■ **This part of the Eagle nebula is named "the spire." It is one well known location where stars are formed or "born." Thousands of stars are formed there. The Eagle nebula is about 7,000 light years away—not far in space terms but a long way for us. The distance from Earth to the Sun is just 8.5 light minutes!**

Gases glow in the light of young stars behind dark clouds

■ DID THE SUN FORM IN A NEBULA?

We think so. It is likely that the Sun and nearby stars all formed together inside a nebula more than 4.6 billion years ago. The young stars were surrounded by whirling discs of dusty material that became systems of planets and moons.

■ WHAT HAPPENED TO THE NEBULA AFTER THE SUN WAS BORN?

The newly-formed Sun and other stars started to pour out heat and light. At first, these young stars were surrounded by a blanket of gas, but eventually their strong radiation pushed the nebula's gases away. As time went on, many of the stars drifted slowly apart.

■ **This is a group of young stars called the Pleiades. If you have good eyesight you might see up to nine of them, but telescopes show about 250. Many are shrouded in gas, which glows with their light.**

■ **This is the** Milky Way galaxy, **the huge spiral of stars to which the Sun (arrowed), and the other stars in this book, belong. The Milky Way is enormous. It is about 100,000 light years across, and contains 200-400 billion stars.**

ARE ALL STARS THE SAME?

No—they are as different as could be, from small and dim to brilliant blue-white, to giants many times bigger than the Sun.

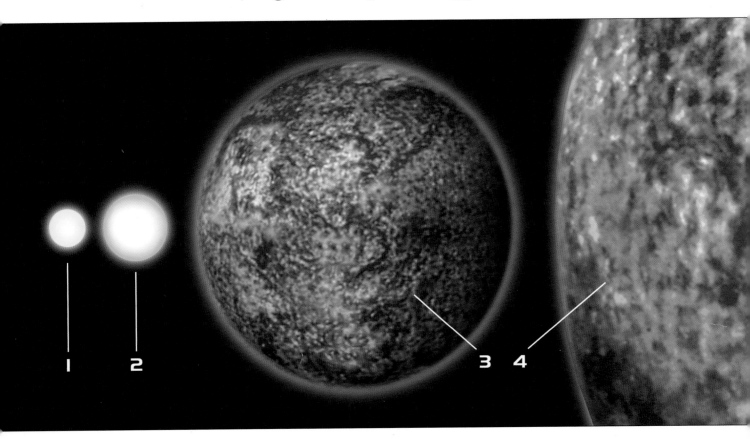

WHY ARE STARS SO DIFFERENT FROM EACH OTHER?

Stars are different because of the amounts of material that come together when they are formed. Stars range in size from small, dense **neutron stars**, which can be 12-25 miles (20-40 km) across, to supergiants like Betelgeuse, which is about 680 million miles (1094 million km) wide.

WOW!
The most common stars in the sky are not very bright at all. They are called **red dwarfs** and are small stars that are cooler than the Sun.

IS THERE AN UPPER LIMIT TO A STAR'S SIZE?

It is about 120-150 times the **mass** of the Sun. If a star has more mass than this, it is likely to become unstable and explode. However, there are some huge stars out there made of very thin gases. If you put the **red giant** Mira in the middle of the solar system, it would fill space as far out as Mars!

■ The color of a star is a guide to its temperature. The coolest stars are the huge red giants. Bluish-white ones are the hottest. The Sun is a medium-heat yellow star.

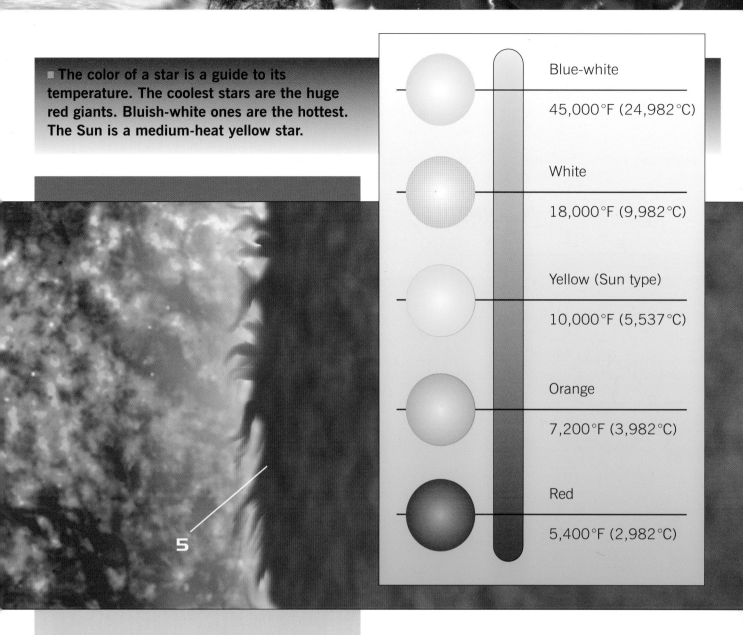

Blue-white

45,000°F (24,982°C)

White

18,000°F (9,982°C)

Yellow (Sun type)

10,000°F (5,537°C)

Orange

7,200°F (3,982°C)

Red

5,400°F (2,982°C)

5

■ Here the Sun (1) is compared with the bigger and brighter Sirius (2). The orange star Pollux (3) is even larger. Dwarfing all three are Aldebaran (4) and Betelgeuse (5).

■ WHICH IS THE BRIGHTEST STAR?

Viewed from Earth, the brightest star you can see is Sirius, which is 8.6 light years away. It is twice as massive as the Sun and pours out 25 times more energy. In fact, there are many brighter stars than Sirius in the galaxy. Those stars are much further away from us, so they do not shine as brightly in our night skies.

■ ARE SMALL STARS ALWAYS HOTTER THAN BIG ONES?

This is often the case, but not always. For example, Proxima Centauri is a small, cool, red dwarf star. Rigel is some 70 times bigger than the Sun, but blazes with a fierce bluish-white light that is about 40,000 times brighter.

WHAT IS IN OUR SPACE NEIGHBORHOOD?

There are more than 70 stars located within 20 light years of us.
Some of them are similar to the Sun, but many more are red dwarfs.

If you could stand on
a planet in the Centauri
system, you would see three
suns in the sky. You would
also have three shadows,
one from each star!

Centauri A (top)
and Centauri B
are bright stars,
easily seen
from Earth

APART FROM THE SUN, WHAT IS THE NEAREST STAR?

The nearest star is the three-star system of Alpha Centauri, which is 4.3 light
years away from us. The biggest and brightest of the three is called Alpha
Centauri A. It is slightly bigger than the Sun. Centauri B is smaller and slightly
dimmer than the Sun. The faint red dwarf star Proxima Centauri is actually
a little closer than either Centauri A or B—it is just 4.2 light years away.

■ WHAT IS THE DOG STAR?

It is another name for Sirius, so-called because it is the brightest star in the **constellation** of Canis Major, the Great Dog (see page 13). Like many stars, Sirius is really a double star. Its smaller companion, Sirius B (arrowed), shines less brightly and is nicknamed "the pup."

■ WHAT IS A BROWN DWARF?

A **brown dwarf** is what is known as a "failed star." It is bigger than a **gas giant** planet like Jupiter, but smaller than a typical star. Brown dwarfs are not big enough for much nuclear fusion in their cores, so they are cooler than normal stars. A typical brown dwarf has a temperature of little more than about 2,000°F (1,100°C).

WOW!
Brown dwarfs are not good vacation spots. Their cloudy surfaces are lashed by storms more violent than anything we have seen in the **solar system**.

As time passes, brown dwarfs slowly cool down. An old brown dwarf may smoulder like an ember at about 660°F (350°C).

■ The nearest known brown dwarfs orbit the orange dwarf star Epsilon Indi, about twelve light years away.

These strange objects circle each other as a pair, while in turn orbiting around Epsilon Indi.

The bigger brown dwarf (above left) has about 45 times more matter than Jupiter. Its surface temperature is just over 1,830°F (1,000°C).

■WHAT ARE THE CONSTELLATIONS?

Ancient astronomers thought they saw star patterns. They named them and told stories about their beginnings. The groups of stars are called constellations.

■ HOW MANY CONSTELLATIONS ARE THERE?

There are 88 constellations, identified by patterns named by the ancient Greeks. Constellations were very important to ancient peoples because they seem to move across the sky with the changing seasons. To ancient farmers, different stars and constellations were guides to knowing when to plant seeds or harvest crops.

■ WHAT'S AN ASTERISM?

This is a star pattern that is not a real constellation. The Big Dipper, or Plough, is probably the most well-known **asterism**. In fact, the Plough is a small part of the constellation Ursa Major, the Great Bear. Other asterisms include the Great Square of Pegasus and the Summer Triangle.

■ Orion is one of the most easily seen constellations. The red giant Betelgeuse (arrowed) marks Orion's shoulder, although you need a pair of binoculars to see the reddish color. Three smaller stars mark Orion's belt.

WOW!
Look for a fuzzy patch below Orion's belt. This is the Orion nebula, a space "nursery" where 700 or so stars are being formed. It is about 1,300 light years away.

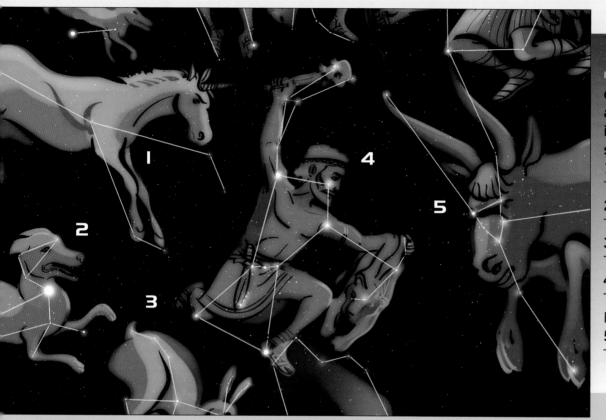

■ These constellations are easily seen in northern skies.
1 Monoceros
The Unicorn
2 Canis Major
The Great Dog
3 Lepus
The Hare
4 Orion
The Mighty Hunter
5 Taurus
The Bull

■ **All stars move through space, but distances are so great and the stars so far away that movement is rarely noticeable. Over a long enough period of time, changes do happen.**

The Big Dipper (below) is shown as it looked 100,000 years ago (1), today (2), and 100,000 years in the future (3).

■ DO THE CONSTELLATIONS MEAN ANYTHING?

Ancient peoples told stories and made legends about these shapes in the sky. For example, Orion was thought to be a great hunter, striding across the heavens with his trusty dog, Canis Major. Orion was said to be driving away the dangerous Taurus the Bull, using a huge club raised over his head.

Orion was a Greek tale. Other ancient civilizations had their own constellations, with other myths and stories to explain them.

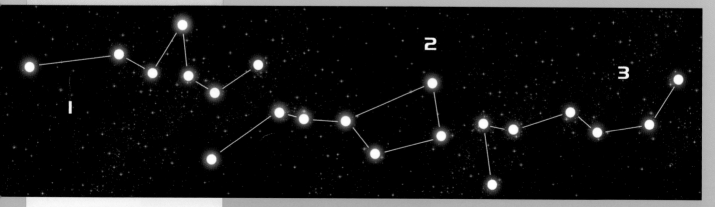

■WHAT ARE DOUBLE AND TRIPLE STARS?

These are stars that move around each other in groups. In fact, single stars such as the Sun are less common, at least in our part of the Milky Way.

■ HOW MANY STARS COME IN GROUPS?

About 60 percent of all stars are not lone stars like the Sun. Instead, they belong to double star (**binary**) or triple star (**trinary**) systems. There are even some star systems made of groups of four or more.

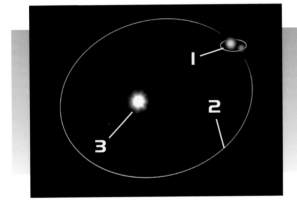

■ This diagram shows a trinary star system. The two smaller stars of the group rotate around each other as a close pair (1). The pair also move in a wide orbit (2), around the bigger, more distant third star (3).
   If the stars are far enough apart, they may each have their own system of planets.

■ CAN I SEE ANY DOUBLE STARS WITHOUT A TELESCOPE?

Some are easy to find. For example, Mizar and its companion Alcor are two stars in the "handle" of the Big Dipper. They are an "optical binary," rather than a true pair of nearby stars. In fact, Mizar and Alcor are about three light years apart—they just happen to look close together, as seen from Earth.

■ Mizar (big star, right) and Alcor are sometimes called the horse and rider. It is possible to see them with the naked eye, but they show up better through a pair of binoculars. Mizar itself is a true binary. It has a small companion, called Mizar B.

■ WHAT IS AN ECLIPSING BINARY?

This is a binary star where one of the two stars passes in front of the other—an eclipse—as seen from Earth. The star Algol is one of these. Its light drops by half every 2.5 days, not because it is varying in brightness, but because it has a cool, dim companion star. When the companion passes in front of Algol, it cuts off some light from our view.

■ Two red dwarfs are the center of a huge dust ring in the Stephenson 34 system, 350 light years away. The gravity of the twin suns has sucked the area around them clear.

This view is from a space rock, clear of the dust ring. In the future, particles in the ring may clump together to form new worlds.

■DO OTHER STARS HAVE PLANETS?

Yes—planets are common across the galaxy. Hundreds of planets have been discovered, although no planets like Earth have yet been found.

■ The star Beta Pictoris has a dust ring in which planets seem to be forming. It could look much like the solar system in its early years.

■ WHAT ARE EXOPLANETS?

It is the general name for any planet outside the Solar System. Most of the **exoplanets** found so far are a lot bigger than Earth. Most are about the size of Jupiter, or somewhat larger. However, an exoplanet orbiting the star Gliese 581 could have something in common with Earth. It may have oceans, like our own planet.

WOW!
The first exoplanets were only discovered in 1992. Since then, research has shown that at least ten percent of Sun-like stars seem to have planetary systems.

■ HOW CAN WE SEE EXOPLANETS?

Exoplanets are so far away that very few of them can be seen through a telescope. Instead, planet-hunters look for tiny movements of the parent stars called wobbles, caused by the gravity of unseen planets.

■ **There is room in the galaxy for all sorts of planets. One of the main aims for astronomers is to find a "new Earth," with seas, air, and—maybe even alien life.**

■ WHERE IS THE NEAREST EXOPLANET?

This is a planet called Epsilon Eridani b, and it is 10.5 light years away, or almost next door as star distances go. The name comes from its parent star, the "b" meaning that it is the second planet of that star.

■ **The 150 light year-distant star HD209458 is a "solar twin", one that is similar to the Sun.**
   Its planet Osiris orbits just 4.4 million miles (7 million km) away. That is close enough to give Osiris a scorching surface temperature of more than 1800°F (982°C).

HOW LONG DO STARS BURN FOR?

Sun-type stars burn steadily for billions of years. Today's Sun is thought to be about 4.6 billion years old, yet is only a middle-aged star.

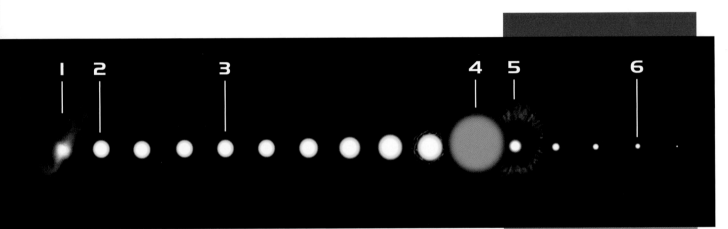

1   2   3   4   5   6

WHEN DOES A SUN-TYPE STAR DIE?

Quite simply, when its hydrogen fuel runs out. This happens when the hydrogen is converted to helium during billions of years of nuclear fusion in its core.

WOW!
About six percent of all stars in our local space zone are white dwarfs. They slowly cool down and get fainter over time, as their stored heat leaks into space.

The star's core will then collapse on itself, while the outer layers heat up, and billow out to form a much bigger red giant star.

A yellow dwarf star is formed within a nebula (1). The young star burns brightly (2). After billions of years burning steadily (3), its outer layers expand to form a huge red giant (4). The red giant blows its outer layers into space (5), leaving a white dwarf, which cools down (6), over billions more years.

In five billion years, early morning on our planet could look like this. The Sun will be a red giant, 100 times bigger than today. The oceans have boiled away and the atmosphere will be gone. In the far future, Earth will be an airless, scorched cinder.

The Eskimo planetary nebula formed about the same time as the Cat's Eye nebula

■ The Cat's Eye planetary nebula is about 1,000 years old, an eyeblink as star ages go. This picture was taken through special filters to show the complex patterns of gas and dust that are still expanding through space.

■ WHAT IS A PLANETARY NEBULA?

A planetary nebula marks the last stage of a red giant, and should not be confused with the much larger nebula in which the star formed billions of years before. Red giants have a short life. After only a few million years, the wispy outer layers are blown away into space. The star's shrunken core is all that remains. It is a strange object, called a white dwarf. It is about the size of a small planet, but with matter so crushed together that a spoonful would weigh a ton!

■HOW POWERFUL IS A SUPERNOVA?

A supernova **is a huge star explosion. It can give off as much energy in a few hours as the Sun has done in billions of years.**

■ This is the Crab nebula, the glowing remains of a supernova that was seen in the year 1054 by Chinese and Arab astronomers.

The gases have been expanding ever since. Today, they cover an area about eleven light years across.

■ COULD THE SUN BE A SUPERNOVA ONE DAY?

No—Sun-type stars are not big enough. The Sun, and any star up to about nine times its mass, will end up as a white dwarf. A supernova is the violent core explosion of a really massive star. When its core shatters, the star's end is quick. It explodes in a searing energy burst that can outshine an entire galaxy for weeks or months, before slowly fading away.

WOW!
A nova is a smaller star explosion. If a white dwarf has a companion star, it may suck gases away from it. These may then be blown off in one or more flares.

The Veil nebula is the delicate remains of a star that went supernova about 7,000 years ago.

Supernovas do have a good side. These gassy waves may compress the thin gases in space between the stars. When this happens, it sets off a new burst of star formation.

Our own Sun and Solar System were probably formed in this way. Earth and everything on it is made of material that exploded from an ancient dying star.

ARE THERE MANY SUPERNOVAS?

Supernovas are quite rare. There is only one every 50 years or so in the entire Milky Way galaxy. Scientists also look for supernovas in other galaxies.

WHAT HAPPENS TO NEARBY PLANETS?

The blast wave from a supernova is strong enough to turn anything nearby instantly into cinders. Gases from the explosion carry on expanding into space at 20,000 miles per second (30,000 km/sec) or more.

This supernova (arrowed) was spotted in a distant galaxy in 1994. It is thought to be a type of supernova where a white dwarf has grown by sucking in material from a binary companion star.

HOW SMALL IS A NEUTRON STAR?

A neutron star forms from the core of a supernova. It packs more matter than the Sun into a sphere just a few miles across.

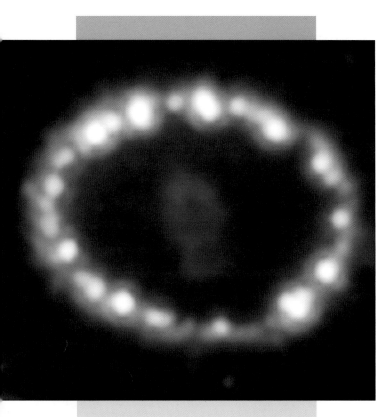

■ These sparkling diamonds of light show the glowing remains of a supernova that exploded more than 160,000 years ago. The ring is thought to have a neutron star in the middle.

■ WHAT HAPPENS AFTER A SUPERNOVA EXPLOSION?

The core of a Sun-type star shrinks to form a planet-size white dwarf. The massive core of a supernova shrinks much smaller than a white dwarf. It may turn into a small object called a neutron star.

■ CAN A NEUTRON STAR CHANGE ITS SIZE?

In a neutron star, all the matter of a big star's core is squashed into a ball no bigger than a fair-sized tropical island. It is a fast-spinning object that can grow over time. If there is a star nearby, the neutron star's gravity can suck material away from it.

WOW!
The first **pulsar**-type neutron star was found in 1967. It was called LGM-1 (Little Green Men-1) at first. For a while, scientists thought it could be an alien radio beacon!

■ HOW MUCH WOULD I WEIGH ON A NEUTRON STAR?

You would not get much of a chance to worry about it, as you would be flattened in an instant. However, the answer is about 67 billion times as much as on Earth. A one pound (0.45 kg) weight on our planet would weigh more than 33 million tons on a neutron star!

■ This is a magnetar, a special kind of neutron star with a magnetic field 1,000 trillion times stronger than that of Earth's.

■ The magnetar is incredibly hot. Its surface is thought to be about 18 million°F (10 million°C).

■ The Vela pulsar is a spinning neutron star that sends out a powerful beam of radio waves and other kinds of radiation. The beam "pulses" or blinks on and off, about eleven times per second, much like a high-speed lighthouse.

■WHAT IS A BLACK HOLE?

A black hole **is a weird space object that has such strong gravity that even light cannot escape. This makes it invisible and explains its name.**

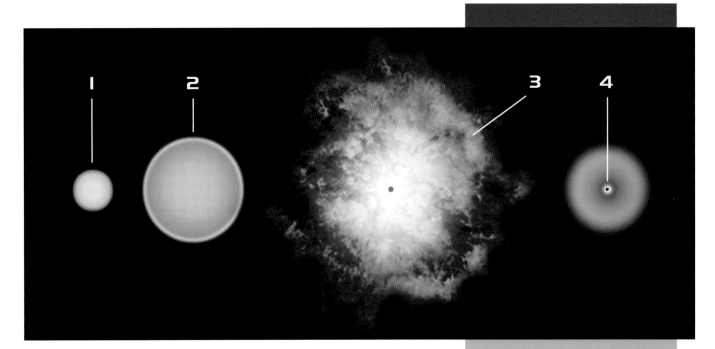

1   2   3   4

■ HOW DOES A BLACK HOLE FORM?

A black hole can result from a supernova explosion. The same core collapse that forms a neutron star occurs, except that now the core shrinks even more, to become a black hole.

WOW!
A black hole would be deadly if you were near it. Luckily, a black hole's gravity affects only the area around it. There are no black holes near Earth.

■ **The birth of a black hole: A massive star (1), burns for billions of years, steadily gaining size with age (2). When its fuel is used up, the star's outer layers are blown off in a supernova explosion (3). The core shrinks, becoming a black hole (4).**

■ SO HOW CAN WE DETECT A BLACK HOLE?

A black hole is a region of space where gravity is so strong that even light is trapped there. Scientists can hunt for black holes by checking the effects they have on space nearby. If there is a star that is close enough, its gases will be sucked away by the black hole, and we can detect this happening. Also, a black hole's super-powerful gravity can distort the appearance of stars behind it.

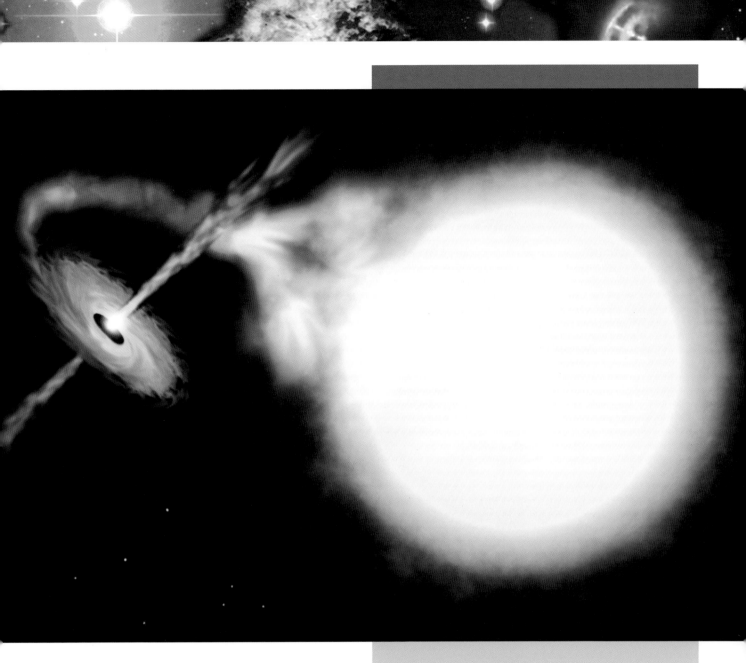

■ IS THERE A BLACK HOLE NEAR OUR SOLAR SYSTEM?

The nearest black hole is thought to be the companion of a star called V4641. They are about 1,600 light years away from Earth.

■ The two-star V4641 system could look like this if you were nearby. The V4641's outer layers are being pulled into the black hole. As the gases approach, they heat up and glow fiercely. They form a spinning disk, while the hole pumps out a powerful jet of radiation.

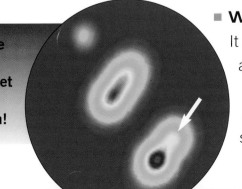

■ V4641's black hole was found in 1999. The bright radiation jet (arrowed) was bigger than the solar system!

■ WHAT IS AN ACCRETION DISK?

It is a spiral of material that can form around a high-gravity object, such as a black hole or neutron star. Such disks are made of gas and dust that is sucked in by the super-strong gravity.

■IS IT EASY TO GO STAR SPOTTING?

You need little or no equipment to get started with simple astronomy. All you really need at the beginning is interest and enthusiasm.

■ DO I NEED A TELESCOPE TO SEE STARS?

While you are learning your way around the sky, a telescope is not much use at all. This is because it shows only a small portion of sky at a time. What you really need is the wide-angle view from your eyes, so you can see as many constellations as possible. That way, you can learn the patterns and shapes quickly and easily.

■ Here is the Plough, not long after a summer sunset.

Note the glowing trail passing through this well-known asterism. It is a high-flying passenger jet, marking its flight path with flashing navigation lights.

Pictures like this are not too difficult to take, but you do need a tripod to keep the camera steady—this exposure took 60 seconds. You have to make sure the tripod is really steady or the picture will be blurry.

■ **Planispheres (1) come in various types. This one is made of tough plastic, so it is ideal to use outside. A computer (2) can show a huge amount of information with software such as Stellarium.**

■ HOW ABOUT A PAIR OF BINOCULARS?

Once you know where to look, binoculars are very handy. They will not make the stars look anything more than points of light, but they do gather a lot of light. Instead of the 3,000 or so visible to your eyes, you will find the sky packed with countless stars.

■ ARE STAR CHARTS USEFUL TO FIND MY WAY IN THE SKY?

An old-fashioned but still useful tool is the planisphere (top). This has an oval window that rotates. Turn it to the correct date and time, and it will show the stars in view that night.

WOW!
Test your eyesight by seeing how many stars in the Pleiades cluster you can see. Then view them through a pair of binoculars. You will be amazed at the difference!

Planetarium software is a modern tool you can use on a computer. One of the best is called Stellarium, and it is free. To use it, enter your place, time, and date. Stellarium will then show the stars, planets, and nebulas that should be visible.

■ **With your eyes only, the Orion nebula looks like a fuzzy patch. With binoculars you should see a little more. However, a view like this needs a powerful telescope.**

■ FACTS AND FIGURES

■ HOW MANY STARS ARE THERE?

The answer is that we do not know for sure, but there are a lot! The Milky Way galaxy, which is about average size, is thought to have 200-400 billion stars. Research shows that there are at least 100 billion galaxies out there. So the total number of stars could be something like this: 10,000,000,000,000,000,000,000!

■ WHAT IS A STAR'S MAGNITUDE?

The apparent **magnitude** of a star is how bright it appears from Earth. Most "naked eye" stars have an apparent magnitude in the range 1 to 6. Each level is 2.5 times brighter than the one below.

Some of the very brightest stars have negative numbers. Sirius, for example, has a magnitude of minus 1.45.

■ NEAREST STARS
Distances shown in light years

1	**Alpha Centauri**	4.3
	Proxima is slightly closer, 4.2 light years	
2	**Barnard's Star**	6.0
	Red dwarf	
3	**Wolf 359**	7.8
	Red dwarf	
4	**Lalande 21185**	8.3
	Red dwarf	
5	**Sirius**	8.6
	Binary system	
6	**Luyten 726-8**	8.7
	Binary system	
7	**Ross 154**	9.7
	Red dwarf	
8	**Ross 248**	10.3
	Red dwarf	
9	**Epsilon Eridani**	10.5
	Young hot star	
10	**Lacaille 9352**	11.7
	Red dwarf	

■ MOST COMMON STARS

These are red dwarfs, or dim stars that are no more than 40 percent of the Sun's size, and have a temperature of only about 4900°F (2700°C).

About two-thirds of all stars near the Sun are red dwarfs. They burn very slowly and will last many times longer than Sun-type stars.

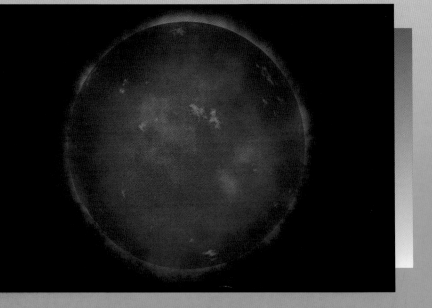

BRIGHTEST STARS

These are the brightest stars in the night sky. Some of them are bright simply because they are near us. Others are much further away. Knowing the distance as well as the apparent brightness allows the actual brightness, or luminosity, to be worked out.

		Magnitude	Distance (in light years)
1	Sirius	-1.45	8.6
2	Canopus	-0.73	1170
3	Alpha Centauri	-0.10	4.3
4	Arcturus	-0.06	36
5	Vega	+0.04	26
6	Capella	+0.08	45
7	Rigel	+0.11	800
8	Procyon	+0.35	11.5
9	Achernar	+0.48	120
10	Beta Centauri	+0.60	525

HOTTEST STARS

Zeta Orionis is a hot blue supergiant star, also called by its Arab name, Alnitak. It is a triple star system about 800 light years away, in the constellation Orion.

Alnitak is easy to spot, as it is the left-hand star of the three that form Orion's belt. In this picture, Alnitak is the very bright star on the left.

You can also see two nebulas in the picture. Below Alnitak is the Flame nebula, and to its right is the Horsehead nebula, one of the best known of all.

WHAT ARE STAR TYPES?

Stars are classed into a number of types according to their temperature. The hottest blue giants are Class O, ranging through B, A, F, G (Sun type stars), K and M (red dwarfs). White dwarfs have a separate D class.

■GLOSSARY

Here are explanations for many of the terms used in this book.

■ Accretion disks are often made from gases pulled from acompanion stars by a neutron star or a black hole.

Accretion disk A disk of dust and gas that circles a high-gravity object, for example, a neutron star or black hole.

Alien The name for life that might exist on planets other than Earth.

Asterism Pattern in the sky that is not a constellation, for example, the Big Dipper, or Plough.

Atom Basic building block of nature, from which everything is made.

Binary, trinary Stars that are grouped in twos or threes.

Black hole A space object with gravity so strong that light cannot escape from it.

Brown dwarf A "failed star," mid-way in size between a gas giant planet and a small star.

Constellation One of 88 star patterns in the sky, named by the ancient Greeks and Romans.

■ A nebula is made of vast quantities of gas and dust. This one is called the Orion nebula.

Core The center of a star, where energy is produced.

Exoplanet A planet of a star other than the Sun.

Gas giant A large planet made mostly of gases, with no solid surface. Jupiter is a gas giant.

Gravity The force of attraction between all objects. Massive objects have a stronger gravitational pull than smaller ones.

Helium The second lightest element, which is also the second major material in a star.

Hydrogen The most common substance in the Universe and most important part of a star's makeup.

Light year The distance that light covers in a year, traveling at a speed of 186,000 miles per second (300,000 km/sec).

Magnetar A type of neutron star with a super-powerful magnetic field.

Magnitude The brightness of a star, as seen from Earth.

Mass The amount of material that makes up an object.

Milky Way galaxy The huge spiral of stars to which the Sun belongs.

Nebula A cloud of gas and dust in outer space.

Part of the Sun to the same scale as the planets

1 2 3 4   5   6   7   8

☐ Here are the Sun and major planets:
1 Mercury
2 Venus
3 Earth
4 Mars
5 Jupiter
6 Saturn
7 Uranus
8 Neptune

Neutron star The collapsed core of a star that is much larger than the Sun.

Nuclear fusion Energy caused by hydrogen fusing under pressure at a star's core to form helium, giving off energy in the process.

Orbit The curving path a space object takes around a more massive one.

Photosphere The visible, glowing surface of a star.

Pulsar A spinning neutron star that sends out a flashing, or "pulsing" beam of radiation.

Radiation The range of wave energy in nature, including radio waves, heat waves, x-rays, and visible light.

Red dwarf A small, dim, very common type of star.

Red giant A future stage of a Sun-type star, when it will expand to become far bigger than it is today.

Solar system The name for the Sun, the eight major planets, and other space objects that circle it.

Supernova The huge explosion of a dying massive star. For a few weeks or months, a supernova may outshine an entire galaxy, until it gradually fades from view.

White dwarf The small, hot remains of a Sun-type star, after its red giant period. Eventually, the white dwarf will cool off, to become a cold, dark, black dwarf.

■ **GOING FURTHER**

Using the Internet is a great way to expand your knowledge of the night sky, stars, and space.

   Your first visit should be to the site of the U.S. space agency, NASA. Its site shows almost everything to do with space, from the history of spaceflight to astronomy, and also plans for future missions.

   There are also websites that give detailed space information. Try these sites to start with:

www.nasa.gov   A huge space site.
www.space.com   Space news site.
www.stellarium.org   Here you can download
                      software that shows the
                      night sky on a computer.

■INDEX

Printed in the U.S.A.—CG